*For Judy
who became
poetry
over BBQ*

Of Course,
I Could Be Wrong

Len Germinara

ISBN: 0692231161
ISBN-13: **978-0692231166**

"G. I. Jake" and " Uh Huh!" in *Everything's Jake* Copyright © 2002 by the author, reprinted with permission from the author.
"Brautigan" in *Dust Bunnies* Copyright © 2003 by the author, reprinted with permission from the author. *Winner of the 2003 Cambridge Poetry Award (Best Narrative Poem)*
"The Four Seasons of Super Heroes" in *Look! Up In The Sky!* Copyright © 2007 by the author, reprinted with permission by the author.
"Endangered Species Monitor" and "Sometimes at Sundown" in *Poems So Far* (Moors Poetry Collective) Copyright © 2012 by MPC; reprinted with permission by the author.
"Nepeta" and "Minor Imposition" in *Lemon Hummus and Other Stories* (by the Moors Poetry Collective) Copyright © 2013 by MPC; reprinted with permission by the author.

"Hospital and Recipe Exchange #1 with Anjali Dhar

CONTENTS

ACKNOWLEDGMENTS

I wish to thank Sarah Oktay, the UMass Boston Nantucket Field Station, and the Moors Poetry Collective. ILYSCB

Proposal

I say to her
     In passing

It might be good if
I take a year off

Get my manuscript together

You know

Concentrate
     Adding
Of course, I might be wrong

Endangered Species Monitor

Awake to this

Crow
First morning caw
Eyes clouded over
I fear not
Here
Fog happens

I'm home
Sitting cross legged
Dune for my bed
Grass painting sand
Invisible
The gentle tip

When words are never enough
The child in me always
Wants more

Wild this is
Mild
I am not

Shoal of empty limpets
For my pillow
Seals
Not sheep
Surf the lullaby of my heart

Beat
Sleep all night
Awake to this

Inclement

When the angle of a gale
Whistles down nor' and east
We hunker down
Wrapped up in our love of each other

What else can we do but

Batten every hatch
Brew strong coffee
Break out the playing cards and cribbage board

Follow the track of shingles and roofing as they go airborne
Like Dorothy watching Elmira Gulch pedaling Toto
To his intended demise
Let that be a warning to all pooches
Everywhere

Fear not puppies
Fill every pot with water
To be sure

Find someone to cuddle with
The minute you hear the weather's gone bad
Surrender to a simpler time
The dog will be alright
There is no one behind the curtain
Really

Read a good book by candlelight
Write to a loved one on foolscap in longhand
Count your blessings

To the banging of shutters against the window frames

From My Shotgun Shack

Yesterday
from my perch
overlooking Folger's Marsh

I watched
with abject horror
a kiteboarder
using that fragile habitat
for mindless recreation

Watched as he struck
a cormorant
never missing a beat
he kept on going

This morning I found that bird
wing ripped and useless

No longer able to feed
it will be meat
certain as the
Sun comes up

Soon it will be duck season

This poem is a warning
For that kiteboarder

Rise

The puddle
By the little beach house
Alive

Water percolating
Astronomical high tide
As animas

Births
One large bubble
Three small

Whirl about
Isopods of air

Coalesce in
Life's continuance
Or not

It's all pressure
And bursting bubbles

I hesitate
A moment

Before

The inquisitive boy
I am at heart

With my old man
Walking stick
Plugs the vent

To see what comes next

To the First Light

I rest my head
When my day stops spinning
Saltmarsh ferris wheel

Time is light

Washes everything awake
Marches east to west

Here is eastern most

Rise up as red cedar in spring
Lie down as long needle pine cones

Sleep through the winter

Wind carries fog in loving arms
Wraps around everything

This morning

Catches on the flotsam
Covers the stones

I am jetsam

Waiting on the fire
Rain extinguish me

Before the sun can catch my damned failing eyes
Shedding tears for my mortality

Another day

Sometimes at Sundown (forever)

He comes down to the water
In gold flashes and
Jesus light

Slow movement
Through green briar

He's the amber
In which he freezes

Ear twitch
A breeze
Through tall grasses

Thirst
Sets him in motion

I wait in the reeds
With cotton mouth

Take the shot

This is a plate of venison tenderloin
Harvested just before sundown
Two days previous

One shot was all it took

The wild mushrooms that serve as garnish
Sautéed in the rendered fat

The smell
Surrounds us
A good book and
Brandy happy

However

Sometimes at sundown
We pass up the shot with bow
Take out our camera

Parched

The faucet needs work
each glass of water dispensed
rends the washer down a
bit

more

Can't place a value
it's easy slake
I'm washed out and slack

Sweat beads on my brow
makes sheets a swampy morass
pad to the fridge

Open it for arctic
respite
tantalizingly brief

Put some ice in the dog's water dish
step outside
hope for a breeze

Triple 8

Sometimes at sunrise
When the smallest of creatures
Roam the earth as giants
In small shoes and
Leave DNA not deciphered like
Alien striations in the sand I see
Foot prints at the lee
And feel you Grey lady
Your ennui palpable

I hear you Yoho
On your way home
From a night on the town
Smell your fur damp
See your eyes glow
Try to forget you
Forget you
Ignore you wrack line
You know
Sea glass still rough
I send you back
Sand dollar cracked
Angels all gone
Sundown is pastel

Sunrise is a wastrel
Covered in sand
My morning walk
On Nantucket

Postcard

Sun sets
A rattle of bird sounds
And bug buzz

Surrounded by water
Sweating beer in the cooler
The vortex of contentment

Here in my lawn chair
Unfettered
With my dog by my side
Bound by affection

We wait for Sarah to come home
from work
she would do
for free

I put up my camera
My pen, my paper

It's time to cook supper

Soon

Daffodils and other
Harbingers
Pop up from winter slumber
All chlorophyll

While we ride
Lawn mowers
Apocryphal monsters all

Sit outdoors
Swat midge flies
Like horse's asses

Sip lemonade
Not quite sweet enough
Make faces

Watch the sun go down
A bouncing red rubber ball

Grill hamburgers or road kill
Chill beer
Till it sweats aluminum
Lose laundry
Unencumbered

Play volleyball for the joy of movement
Go swimming backwards towards creation

Soon

Posted: No Swimming

July leaves

Evidence of life
Littering the wrack line

Dead things whispering
An aside to the
Heat astride my chest
The stench in my nose

This is the month
I like least

Its deer flies and allergens
Everything grabs, trips or
Cuts you
Wants something
Draws bull's-eyes on babies bottoms

And still they come

The idle on vacation

People ask us all the time, "What Do You and Sarah Do for Fun on Nantucket?"

When seen from above
Nantucket may appear to be
A bloated tick
Like the one we have here

Let's place it
Under our microscope

After we've run through fields
of wild grasses
just before sunrise

A white sheet dragged behind
To gather specimens

Even though we're in the midst
Of prolonged drought conditions

Our feet are
Covered in dew

Tonight
Our work done
We'll check each other

Thoroughly

For hitchhikers

Does this answer your question?

FIGAWI

For every maw aflutter
wanting wine and
sailboat races

To every horse
in
a race not run
let slip the traces

May it rain on
your outdoor activities
pop the breaker
too much plugged in
not enough power

Storm warnings
FIGAWI
buy a postcard
gather up your beach chairs
grab your children's hand
go home

really.

The poet as a young man

In the dark
Ill-defined corridors of
Pillows and night sweat
I see your face
Plead for forgiveness
That does not come

Awake once more
I
Pull on my clothes

Morning shakes my trousers
Looking for the price
Of a cup of coffee

Here in this hotel that
Rents by the hour, day, week
Whatever time you can afford
Whatever time you have left
Once young

A baseball card
Slapping against the spokes of
The bicycle
You got on your 10th birthday

And other things
That fall from your pocket

Tiger Balm Situation

Today is Tuesday
Two days later
Still I ache

Monday was every bit
As malicious
Muscles unable to speak
Have no mouth
But must scream

And I can't remember
Her name

Sunday is desolate
Barstools empty

Baseball on the TV
Barflies on the nod

Beer still warm
Just placed in the cooler

You get five songs
For two bucks
From the jukebox here and
When I'm drinking
I've been known to get silly so

I put four dollars in
Play Free Bird
10 times

I wait for the guitar solo
Before I attempt
My fade away

I burst through barroom doors and
The light of the world
Is lenient

My remaining brain cells
Penitent
It's then that I recall her name

She said her name was
Dandelion
Just before she slipped
The sandals off her tiny painted feet
And placed them in my lap
Pleased to meet you was my reply
Dandelion tells me she likes to cook

I comment that
It's nice to know she's not just
A pretty face

She smiles
Says feel my legs

I just shaved this morning

Today is Tuesday
Two days later
And I still ache

Whatever became of him?

We are born of turgescent particles with
Seemingly little rhyme or reason.
Caught up and transcribed by the minutiae
That carries us from season to season.
Semi-precious moments strung together and
Remembered through photographs and synapses misfiring.
I try to recall with exactitude the arms
That held us close
The year
And the circumstance that brought us together
In the first place.
I am the forgotten name in so many family albums.
The silly fool that danced a tarantella, poorly,
The day you were married and
Was never heard from again.
I'm never far from that place of transgression.
My life is, for the most part static.
Yet, I'm light years from where you are now.
Wondering how life has treated you since.
Do you sometimes try to recall and wince?
When your children,
In a moment of primeval remembrance, say my name
Ask you where I went
And why

For Joe and His Beat up Motor Scooter

Hey Joe hang up the colors for now
The ones with the picture of Ginsberg
Kerouac and Burroughs on the edges

As beat as your old scooter
With its faded paint
And worn out tires

Never really beautiful but
She does keep the rubber on the road

And the seat is well worn
Evidence of two asses

The peg is bent

Which indicates as well as anything
The reason why they call it dope

Put a tarp down in the living room
It's time to strip the engine
Pull the carburetor
Rework the timing

While you're at it
Re-chrome the pipes
Give her a new coat of paint

But leave the peg bent
As a reminder

Have her ready for a putt
Come next spring

Labor Day

From our house overlooking the Merrimac
Mother and I would walk
To father's work
On payday

The men would crowd the windows at noon
Hung like lanterns
Cigarettes stitched their lips tight
Stoic parchment waiting on
The first beer of the day
Cookout on the weekend

Work in rows of sweat and chemicals
Quietly placing one minute
Next to the lastings

Stacked in gross lots
For mass consumption
That ultimately and indiscriminately kills
Even your will to live

Middle class
Or upper lower class
Self-loathing cogs in a wheel

With a house
Never really owned

Second hand car
Hand-picked by
An uncle who had worked in the motor pool
His stint in Korea

We vacationed in Maine
Mackerel and harbor seals
Before lunch
Road side stands

Shopping for curios and moccasins
Into the ice cream sunset

One week a year

Memory of a Bouncing Ball

I should remember his name
I don't

Met him at a yard sale
My ex and I hosted

The kind that pays
For legal costs and other niceties
Associated with the dissolution
Of joint property

Suffice it to say
Mental anguish and chemical imbalance
Account for memory loss of particulars
In this circumstance

I should remember his name

Not just some vague recollection
His height
That he wore glasses
We played racquetball together
I joined his club

I should remember his girlfriend's name
The nurse

Who hovered over him
When he
From time to time
Would pass out briefly
After a game or two

She'd shoo all away
Saying it happened all the time
And he didn't want anyone to fuss

He'd be fine

I think his name was Mark

An offhand comment made me think of him

Saturdays Gramps would come for a walk
In the woods where we lived
Back in the 60's

Must have been
The year he died

I have no memory of him
After that year
Except his funeral

He'd get out of his car
And go
Hardly stopping to say a word
To any of us
Hounds at his heels
Stogie in his pie hole

Just as well
He wasn't altogether pleasant

Prone to starting arguments
And flatulence
On his good days

A wisp
Of smoke
And pained expression
Taking a walk
In the woods

That was gramps

Heading out

No one ever said
They hated to see him go

Until he was gone

Ring around the Moon

"Call no man happy until he is dead" – Herodotus

Know this brother, sister, whomever.
I have slept with the monster of beginning's womb,
suffered the effluvium and suffocation of certain consequence,
wobbled as newborn under the harsh light of what is and
Wondered, why? We all have.

My gnarled arthritic sensibilities are
Searching for a way to unbutton
The pockets of your conclusion.

Turned off by zeroes and ones,
Because math is not my strong point
And I so want this equation to make sense to you.
I sharpen my pencil, write this longhand,
take out my calculator.

Knowing full well that a ring around the moon
Is a moon bow (which is not technically correct) and
Something that I would have you see
before you go,
If going is what you must do.

For you who know Herodotus is happy now
Call me so we may explore this paradox
Look up in the sky and wonder why
in a new light.

We'll take out our slide rules and our stop watches
That we might realize the so much more
A salient point just beyond

Because that counts for something

The other side of that moon is dark
But we could find illumination
Obsidian, listen to the music of another morning
And find joy.

All My Pretty Poems

I've been mowing wild grasses
With alliterations and
Iris contractions
Hotter than August
Slower than molasses

More important to me than you ever were

I'm clearing away
Evidence of you
Filling in the vernal pools that were your eyes
Tossing all in the dumpster of a new day

It's spring and more than time

I'm surfing on a wave of lead
And organic matter
That's one part anticipation
Two parts dread and
Suppurating

Because you are an invasive species
I cut you out with fervor
A zealot straight razor

Writing this in cursive
My ink spittle and blood

You are dogma scraped from my shoe
I'm so happy to be done with you

But no hard feelings
I wish you well

And here am I a flagellant
Inured of the pain
Impervious to the voices

In my head
Saying
Take a moment
Reassess the situation

My wounds will be cauterized
Tears will keep the area irrigated
Enough
to let healing begin

I hope

You're still irritated
Good

I won't miss you
Because you never walked
In front of my car

I won't remember you
I won't notice
The millions of tiny scars
You left

I'm not that introspective

Vacation Contemplation

This morning, the wife and I
Babbling over morning ablutions
Knee deep in snowdrifts
Books and paper everywhere
Doing the two-step around our animals,
Each other
Living in close quarters bed bug crazy

We need an assassination vacation
Riding the crazy train of ennui are we
Require a karmic high colonic
It's the only way to combat our cabin fever

So we've packed our baseball bats and our ball peen hammers
Smile on our face, the knowing we've made the right choice

Howl, we HOWL BUG-EYED
We'll feed some yuppie buckwheat's
The first chance we get

We'll giggle like school kids as the bones crack
Toss the worms a gooey slop

This is our murder of crows
Very Italian/Turkish this thing of ours
A marinara on the simmer
A cauldron on the boil

We'll send you a postcard

Finding a Bookstore

Traveling leads to bookstores for us,
no matter where we go, books stalk us. Find us in some
back alley at the turn of the century,
game afoot.

These mythic fields wherein time is laid waste,
Cerulean funerary spores await a stiff wind.
piled high, stacked supplicants set against an indifferent
child's opinion.

We probe the fathomless depth of our
desire for the as yet, unread,
great American novel of the last 50 years.

We are the ammonia explosion,
a Leonid meteor in the windowed reflection that grasp for
the light behind the fire.
Aurora Borealis the muffler around our necks, the clips
that hold our mittens.

I know your breath's rhythm, purring,
lying so close to me, in me.
Amongst these back pages the limitless un-read
Waiting.

These are the days of nights that
lead me down a narrow hall, page turning
to your face when the moon is upon it;
touch your cheek, a wisp of tomorrow,
capricious as a baby's laughter.
This is the where, when we travel, we are holy;
most wholly we.

All the pictures I took came out blurry

Swung a wide loop through Texas
Down through Mexico
In a time when
Something yellow was blooming
A ribbon in your hair
Pony soldier woman

Stopped at a reservation smoke shop
looking for Quanah Parker's
tobacco pouch and
postcard pictures of Wild Bill

Something to write about

Let the folks back home know
We're as close to relaxed
As it ever gets
On an inter-state highway
At 80 miles an hour

We've been listening to an audio book
Cause radio died here
with Jesus on the cross
next to it
Now everybody suffers

It's Easter Sunday
We're not going to
Try finding a place to stop and eat
We're
Drinking roadhouse takeout coffee
Chewing on Elk jerky
Listening to
Keith Richards
Life story

Keep driving

Have yourself a very surreal Christmas

Sarah and I attempt to repair the tear
In our time continuum
With a yearly pre-Christmas sojourn south

Living as we do
With our hair on fire
From first light
Until last meteor
Riding the running boards of this
Threadbare science platform
"Field Station"

We hope it holds
The time we're away
Toss some salt over shoulder
Fingers crossed

We won't look back to witness
What might be exploding
In the rearview mirror

There comes a time
When you just can't care
Another moment
Without losing your mind

McDonough

You should know we'll think of you
Every time we check the maps
Bought at that Oklahoma
Reservation gas station

Last year

The attendant told us that day
We might buy the book and never

Own the contents

I told him
Shut up
Or words to that effect

And smile every time
I re-tell the story

This current trip has
Taken on the fragility of thin ice

Crisscrossed by power lines
Looking for an oasis

The tortured spaces need filling

Up ahead stands a bindle stiff
Thumb in the wind

Ecstatic magician or
Coyote vagina

Not known - Unknowable

We stop
Offer her a ride.

Bourbon Street Tomorrow

We boarded the train
in the dark
Cold dragon's breath
Mid-winter vortex

Boston to NOLA
Holes in our
Spanish leather

Sleet raking us
On the long walk
To our sleeper car

Where
Thankfully our
Beds are already turned down

This is a work in progress
We'll need our rest

A day and a half by train
Just the ticket

The fading shadows applause
Reflecting on the window pane
In Pennsylvania

Everything else falls away
to the end of the line
Where jazz and oysters
Await us

I Believe in Circular Rotation

The snow comes a mute swan to cover my feet
Of grey clay
to be rendered down when the weather warms
A puddles indentation's
briefest mention in a drought
Laugh like rain my days diminution
Day tripper in a Somerset South Sea story
Dance for a sixpence
without pants
Ignore the ignominious
as they you
Tip your hat to the swell in the deep end
Hold your nose against the din and
all that that entails
Entrails and garden path's lead you astray
Wink of a ponytail
Swishing hey how you doing
It warms
midafternoon light flickers on
Reflective surfaces distorts all images
Real or imagined in sleeps recesses
A nap most welcome
settle for a quick smoke
Turn off the cell phone unplug the computer
yank
Throw the modem over your shoulder for good luck
Hang your socks over the radiator
slip on a disk
Play some NOLA Gris-Gris
Tom Tom and Tambourines
Leave your hat on the turntable spinning

Brautigan

Richard and I went fishing Monday.
We stopped at Willard's Market,
for smokes, worms, and some Kool-Aid.

Richard had offered to pay.
As usual, Richard only had Monopoly money
little scraps of paper with hand drawn fish
So I gave the attendant $4.00 for a $3.99 purchase.

Worms, we couldn't afford
so we used Kool-Aid,
sat lazy fishing at our river
for the better part of an afternoon.
Toes in the mud,
fish beginning to rise.

I've known Richard for years,
but to be his lover is completely awesome with a capital A,
mouth open,
eyes squeezed tight.
Ah.....

Richard once compared lazy fishing
to loading mercury with a pitchfork.
He often tells me in the afterglow,
breath short,
eyes wide, I see the heavy water rise and I'm gone.

We fish at the North River,
right next to the old mill.
You know the place.
We set about our task
the Kool-Aid slides on the hook smooth.
Everything seems suspended in watermelon sugar.

We didn't catch a fish that day.

I don't know why Richard calls me Trout.
My name is Amy.
He just started calling me Trout one day when we was fishing
And it just stuck.

We was on vacation.
Lake Winnipesaukee, I think.
It was fall and I felt like a rainbow,
now Trout's my name.

Richard used to be famous
to hear him tell it.

It was before I met him.
He said he was considered a humorist.
Funny, nothing he's ever said or done has struck me as funny.

He owns a black cat.
Richard calls him Dogfood.
He often gives the cat's name as an example of his humor.
If you ask me, that ain't funny.
I think it's kind of sad.
I think Richard's sad,
but I love him.

He makes me feel weak and alive all at once.
I don't much understand him,
my education is lacking and he's an educated man.

He never makes me feel lacking though,
And I can almost see the stars as he sees them
in the sound of his voice.

Maybe I'm too casual.
One last remnant of the summer of love.
Long, straight hair.
Bell bottom jeans, Frye boots.
The day we met I said
Richard, I hide the keys to my apartment under the doormat
let yourself in.

I sleep heavy.

He showed up that night like a sombrero that fell from the sky.

Afterward, we lay as crumpled as the linen under us.
Just like that.
I remember thinking, what the hell happened?
It's always like that with Richard,
maybe not quite as hot,
but better than a slap on the ass.

That was the first time he ever slapped me on the ass.
I like it when he does it,
even when I pretend not to like it.
Believe me, I can pretend good.

I told Richard, "I see stars in your voice."
he looked at me like he saw fire for the first time,
but he stayed rooted.
He didn't run.
Richard's not a running man,
at least not the Richard I know,
knew.......

There is never enough time for fishing,
even if fishing is all you have to do.
Fame is a clever trick much like the wonder of a photograph.
I have a photograph of Richard and me.

We set up a camera on a log by our favorite spot.
Fell into focus wrapped in each other's arms.
The timer whirred,
and snapped our shot.

Richard said "Trout,
I love it here with you,
remember that whenever you look at this picture."

The picture of Richard and me hangs in my parlor,
right next to Richard's empty gun rack.

Faux Olson

Minimums to SBPF, Letter 27 [released]

I come back to the Iconography of it,
Her hair falling to the left
Where her cat sleeps at night
While the dog and I sleep to the   right
And the rest of the world passes by
I'm at home
And buzzed

To the left lies Polpis Harbor
This is as it should be, no?

My memory, and this is apocryphal, I am, as mentioned addled,
Is of an Open House at the UMass Nantucket Field Station
A "meet and greet" to introduce them to Sarah
The new director
Who is now my wife and will always be my inamorata
She spends all that day in the classroom, on the bluff
Explaining water quality and her work at Ground Zero

Then lunch
is served, cold cuts and potato salad
while all sit
and get comfortable

The Chancellor, dressed in her summer finery, her dress red, her
cheeks flushed,
the necklace she wears the finest
Gold, makes her opening remarks

While Frank Spriggs, former Nantucket Selectman,
for kicks calls out from the gathered throng
Let's hear more from Sarah

This is the beginning of the novel, this

Is not coincidence, this,
Grey Lady, is the seminal moment
        It is the dawn of sentience
No longer sated by processions of predecessors
Daffodils and
remember when you could drive on every beach

From where you stand on 'Sconset
Or the West End with the motion of the waves
Tickling your feet
 More than you were

There will be a strict moral order
Your children's inheritance
Secure

        No money can unseat you

A Nantucketer
Is a complex of old world superstitions
Themselves a hexagonal morass
Of nature's preservation
I have no sense, gypsy
        Plus this, minus that
Forever is not
You leaning over the edge
throwing money at a problem
Backwards

I
implore you

Listen to reason

Polpis
        is
This

The Four Seasons of Superheroes

#1

In summer I read Marvel comics
Flashlight and worn blanket
The stars of Alpha Centauri
My Neon soliloquy

I want to be Captain America
Pathos the driving force in my fantasy life
Made real by holding that coarse
Paper with the glossy wrapper
Opposed to reality

I needed someone to spell the sound of a nose breaking
Thank you Stan Lee

#2

In the Fall I visit Valhalla
The gravitational pull inexorable
Thor's THHHWOKK blocked out
In an arch from hip
To point of impact

Most amazed I ever made it this far
I only wanted a shield to ward off bullets
Something to hide behind
While I fired crabapple invectives
At passersby

#3

In winter I met Wonder Woman
On her way to work
All clogs and apple cheeked
Speculative fiction in her wake

Now I ride the passenger jet
I drive a car with a blue "On-Star" button
Carry in the palm of my hand all I need
I beam
I live long
I prosper
Zoom, Zoom…
Zoom

#4

In just spring
We walk the salt marsh
Ancient spoken word
Ankle deep in ooze
Turning over rocks
Looking for new language

Pulling the plumbing of
Poetry's soul
Spring is like a perhaps hand
Mechanically enhanced

Lest We Forget, The World Is
Round Here, And God Says Hah! #1

I used to find succor
In Humor
Lampooning with a mirror
That what we'd only wish
on another

Fiddle me a tune
To tame the savage beast

Born of sugars low
That which takes most

Sugar high that would grasp summer hot
Consequence of little significance

What will find you
Who would sit in front
of your computer screen
to the exclusion
past all others

Will you stare beyond
Through Hubble's telescopic metaphor
See the beginning
Of the end.

Where life takes you
For only God knows what

**Lest We Forget, The World is
Round Here, And God Says Hah! #2**

For only God knows what
Where life takes you

Of the end
See the beginning
Through Hubble's telescopic metaphor
Will you stare beyond

Past all others
To the exclusion
Of your computer screen
Who would sit in front
What will find you

Consequence of little significance
Sugar high that would grasp summer hot

That which takes most
Born of sugars low

To tame the savage beast
Fiddle me a tune

On another
That what we'd only wish
Lampooning with a mirror
In humor
I used to find succor

Pond without a name

Winter gone Bittern
Wades in to last year's
Cattail remnants
Famished Isosceles triangle
In search of a meal
That won't catch in her craw

She doesn't see me coming

Until the camera gives me away
Tiny motors and moving pieces
My shaky hands

Startled
She strikes a pose
Nose straight up in the air
Like sedges ready to scatter seed

Ragged as an old mill saw
Hung on a barn wall

I move closer

She's broken glass
Moving her air frame
Into the wind

One more pose

Before she goes
On with her morning
Somewhere else

Morning Spares Us Nothing

My past comes calling
Each and every morning

Shakes me a ptarmigan
In a wolf's white fangs

My visage bears witness in the mirror
Accident scene picture
Major fender bender

Clearly I've been concussed
A time or two

It matters not to the mutt
Asleep at the foot of the bed
I wake him

He needs to be walked
A working dog

Walking helps
Identify the sore spots

Grab a cane on the way out the door
The one from Costa Rica

Tool around the perimeter
This island on the water

Wake the whitetails asleep
In the tall grass

They'll squawk and stamp their feet
I care not
Why should they be spared?

Scientific Inquiry

Up from the offshore depth
She clouds the water
A harbor obstruction
Tired and ready for oblivion

The Harbormaster alerted
Takes up a wooden boat pole
Old Nantucket lucky
Had it been new money metal
He wouldn't have lived to tell the tale

This is a torpedo ray
Deep water dweller
A shark-like tail
Joined to a hammered flat body
More voltage than an electric eel

Two have washed ashore
In the last year
No one knows why

Scientific enquiry
Requires a necropsy
A rare find brings scientists
Like buzzards after road kill
Hungry for knowledge, circling
Testing with sensory perception
Then the knife

The cartilage like rug matting
Internal organs pastel pink and blue
A sunset postcard from land's end
Story in the paper
Bags in a freezer
All that's left of her
A picture
Poem
An article
And the discussion begins

9 When It Happened

Wunse upon a tyme
I worked as scyintist
When and where
No longer
Matter any more
Scyince is dead
Unforchently

But eye remember
The silver fishes in the flash lites spark
Layt at nyght
Counting Horseshoe crabs
With Sarah and Lenny

Blackberries in July ripe and jucee

Before the market crashes
Hell fire catshes
And the hole wyde world
Was a place

No more
So eye right about it

This warm day in October

We notice wooly bears and
Paper wasps everywhere

Yellow legs and tree swallows
Murmuring

So many blue herons
In one place

I'm compelled
To point them out
  Even though I know
You see them

We decide to take
A kayak trip
Through the marsh
To hunt the best
Photographic subjects

The expensive camera
    My expensive camera
In a ten year old's hands

What was I thinking?

The red knot in my throat
Wants to know

It all works out

He takes a few shots
Anyone would be proud of

And we talk
About things we like

Those we don't like
Brussels sprouts and beets

And what we'll do next
Time

We see wooly bears
And paper wasps everywhere

Hospital - Anjali & Lenny

A view that lasts forever
On the cancer level of Mass General
Big heaters blasting over your head
Sadness tangible in the air
Tropic trees line the hallways
Trying to brighten the mood
Long benches that are hard and blue
A volunteer carting snacks around the waiting room
People rushing around you, but you are oblivious to it
You are focused on the view.

They say
From here
you can see
tomorrow
when the conditions
are just right
but they rarely are
    that being said

it only matters that
you see the one
closest to you
right now

tomorrow is so far
away

and there's so much more to see

Recipe Exchange #1

Lemon Crisp Cookies

"They feel crumbly and smushy,
It smells like lemon in a nice twisted way.
They look scrumptious, fit for a king,
The sound of tiny 'eat me!'s' are emitted from the cookies.
The taste of these delicious cookies are indescribable to mankind."

      -Avacado (Anjali)

Almond Milk Moon

I've heard the sound
of the scrumptious
Late at night
the moon full of almond milk
cats circling my feet

I wipe the crumbly sandman
from my eyes
sit with a plate
of the thing I most appreciate
something sweet

A poem from a friend

      -Lennie

Uh Huh!

With Jake there's always the pre-walk intrusion
A simple muscle reaction
Twitch, Twitch, Twitch

We love the morning
It's almost an elegy
For lost sleep
Yawns stretched tight like strings
On a violin
Screeching tires and dawn's first light

We share in the steam from our breath
A kiss good morning
We wag in unison
Sometimes I share in the water ceremony with him
Lord, what the neighbors must think

Next stop is usually the coffee shop
We hop the jalopy and boogie
Jake digs the plain doughnut holes
I dig the waitress

Both of us dogs

Jake's dog rocket makes me smile every time
I leave a tip

Jake licks the crumbs from the co-pilots seat
It may not seem like much
But we like the repetition
We like it like that, Uh Huh!

This is usually followed by a walk in the woods

Once last spring
On a day shrouded with the early dew
Jake and I found a mother Snapping Turtle

Depositing a clutch of eggs in a sandy embankment

Jake went to heel and I held my breath
The dirt was no match for her primordial imperative
My body an imperfect container for the image and my love for Jake
at that moment

G. I. Jake

We've been watching the aftermath of 9/11
It's 9/13 and the dogs have gone to work

My dog Jake says he wants to enlist
He wants to be all he can be
Jump out of helicopters
Wear a cool uniform
You know, something all the bitches
Will howl for

He got the idea from that movie
My Dog Skip
Jake tells me he would be an excellent G.I. dog
He does this by bringing his muzzle close to my ear
Says SNIFFFF!

I say to him
Jake, in that movie the army rejected Skip
Remember?

He puts one paw over his eyes
Like Petey from "Our Gang"

Yeah, I know
You're thinking
Does he really think his dog talks to him?

NO/YES
Maybe

Be that as it may, the thought of any dog
Working amongst the rubble
Searching for the dead
With a dog's need to please
Saddens me

But only for as long as it takes
For Jake to pull close to my side
I've taught how to high five
And I say give me paw dog
He does every time

I say
I'd like you to do stuff like that forever
But I tell him
Jake, you do what you think is best
I trust your judgment

Minor Imposition

Under a moon most full
Dressed in fluorescent orange

I walk the moors
To look for you
Fur and teeth
Damp bog breath

The wind shakes the bayberry
A rabbit's heart beat
before the death blow

Not properly dressed for the change in weather
My hands reverberate past bone breaks
Sandals
No socks
a mistake

It does not deter me
Find you demon I will

There
on the bluff
I see

No

It's a deer

Damn you
son of a bitch

I'm sleepy

Cannot rest while you roam
Out there in the shadows

Some trigger happy hunter
Might shoot you/me down
Just for the hell of it

I must love you
dog

Dog Walking

My preference would have been death by sleep
But we always accepted whatever paw he offered so
When he needed help crossing over
We got him help
Held him close till his last breath

Moreover it's my own dread of mortality
That holds to the images of his loss of his once keen senses
The knowing after all that life is a diminution

And this is a dream

The stairs once taken in gleeful leaps that became daunting
The hand signals indecipherable and
Dare I say this here?
The incontinence

Unintended sleigh rides down the stairs
Legs a failing folding table
Followed by flatulence

He was the nuzzle at the intersection of legs
That insisted on attention
The one who's head was in my lap
Whenever I needed to know someone was on my side
No matter what

He was redemption
That can never be truly earned
A dog's love is like that

He was the exuberance of an over sugared child
At the end of my working day
When I had little to look forward to

My Shaky Jake

His eyes were the depths of love and
All its consequences that mirrors the twinge I feel and
I will not forget or mourn

He sees nothing and hears less now
But he is forever here in these pages

This will make the looking back
Somewhat acceptable
A calm exhalation as he lies at my feet

This is a celebration
A dream that ends
With a walk

Nepeta

Sun Dial felines sit
Half past noon
Lunatics framed in shadow
Wound up tight
Transfixed by
Marsh Wrens
Perched on the other side of
The sill

Pie-eyed
Carnivores
Caught up in
Euphoria
Fueled by catnip
Planted for ornament

My home is an opium den
For feral Mammalians
Something to entertain them
While I'm away
A windfall

A window somewhere needs to be closed
Explosion of feathers in the corner
Confirms it

How to

It's simply this
Give yourself permission
Open the gates
Let the words out

Choose them

Mourning dove
Marsh wren
Great blue heron

A way to
Hold the place

Open

Allow that Music
To express your delight
In naming a thing
Be
The tune you dance to

Bring the world inside you
From the slant

From your dreams
To the page

A contract you make
In the world
Of imagination

Create a safe space

Where you see a Sycamore
Know what it is

Write it.

Reply to an Epitaph

I live thirty miles out to sea, America
The air is clean and clear
Sunset, a Coney Island of the mind
Not much noise unless you count the shorebirds
Neighbors always finding fault with someone
Keep your children close
Protect their eyes

Where houses sell for millions
Median income unfathomable
I qualify for food stamps
Money poor and rich beyond measure
Conundrum

I now know why folk songs are so often dulcet
Widow walks and ghost talks on Main Street so prevalent

This is a song for Nantucket
Forever in mourning
Absalom Boston and Sarah Skootequary
This is why Plovers face the wind when nesting
They may not make it but they see it coming
Leave little to mark their passing

These are indelible
Lonely Polaroids in an unmarked box

I've watched Xeno's paradox
Sand lifted and spun
Some wild whirl as one beach not earth bound
Not stagnant or immortal we

Come with me next time
Dance the Ghost Dance
Listen to the surf and follow the light
This is a Merry-Go-Round at the edge of oblivion

Somewhere a Luddite is laughing
I am not laughing

ABOUT THE AUTHOR

Poet, Len Germinara has been hosting and performing poetry throughout New England for over three decades. His work has appeared in magazines, anthologies, and six collections of his work. Germinara, and his wife Dr. Sarah Oktay have co-edited numerous anthologies and for the past ten years they have hosted Spoken Word Nantucket.

For contact and other information please visit Len at http://www.lengerminara.com/ or www.spokenwordnantucket.org